I'd Be Your Hero

A royal tale of godly character

Kathryn O'Brien ～ illustrated by Michael Garland

Standard
PUBLISHING
Bringing The Word to Life™

Cincinnati, Ohio

"IF you were a queen, I'd be your hero," said the little boy to his mother.

"**We** would live in a gigantic castle made of heavy stone with high towers and secret lookouts and a deep moat filled with snapping alligators, hissing snakes, and stinging eels," said the little boy. "I would stand guard in the tallest tower to keep watch over our kingdom and make our castle secure."

"Yes," said his mother, "and if you heard a strange noise while keeping watch, you would stand very still and call out, 'Halt! Who goes there?' because you are very brave."

Do not be terrified . . . for the Lord your God will be with you wherever you go.

Joshua 1:9

"**Each** day I would shout, 'ON GUARD!' as Father and I fenced with our shining swords," said the little boy. "And then I would take out my royal bow and arrows to practice archery."

"You would hold your bow very steady and take careful aim," said his mother. "And if your arrows missed the mark, you would keep trying, because you are a hard worker."

Let us run with perseverance the race marked out for us. Let us fix our eyes on Jesus.

Hebrews 12:1, 2

"**We** would have a royal jousting tournament!" said the boy. "I would ride my faithful steed and hold my lance steady and strong as I rode."

"Yes," said his mother, "and you would ride swiftly and skillfully, doing your very best, because you are very talented.

I have filled him with the Spirit of God, with skill, ability and knowledge.

Exodus 31:3

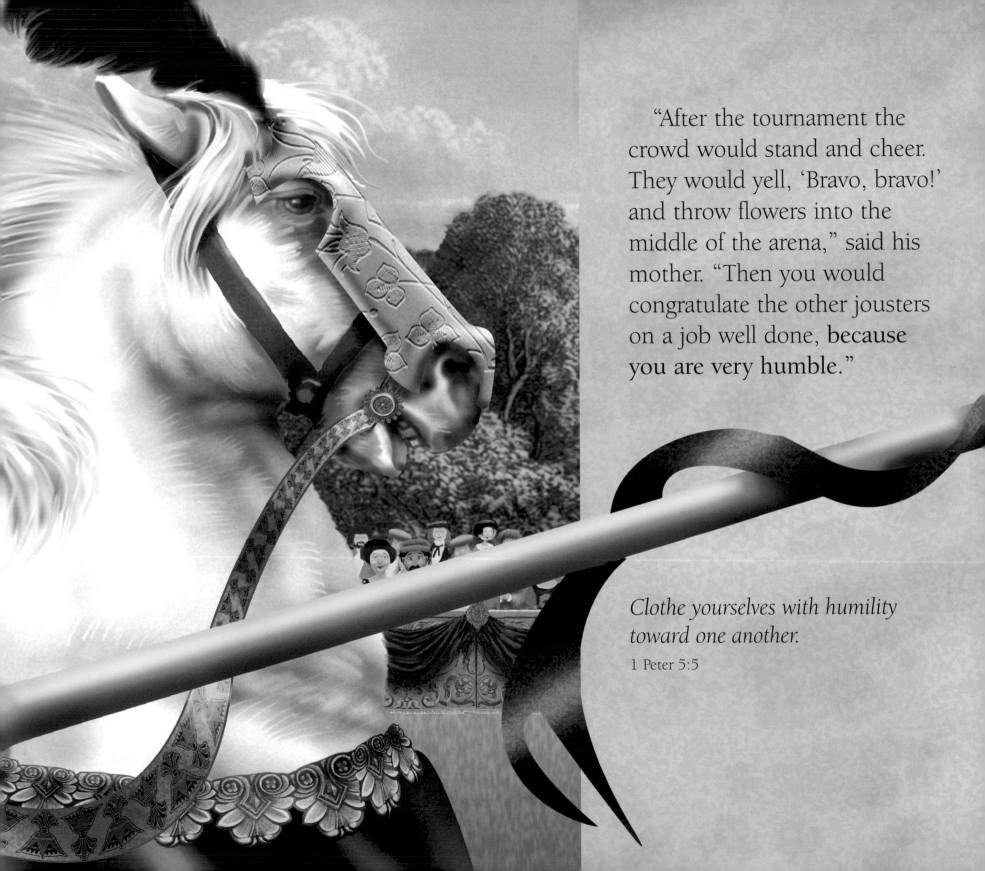

"After the tournament the crowd would stand and cheer. They would yell, 'Bravo, bravo!' and throw flowers into the middle of the arena," said his mother. "Then you would congratulate the other jousters on a job well done, **because you are very humble.**"

Clothe yourselves with humility toward one another.
1 Peter 5:5

"**Father** and I would take great journeys together, running through thick forests and charging over high mountains and leaping across rocky streams," said the boy.

"And on your journeys, Father would ask you which way you thought was best," said his mother, "because you know how to make good choices."

Blessed is the man who finds wisdom.

Proverbs 3:13

"We would find fantastic treasures as we explored – giant furry spiders and long slippery worms, overgrown snails with soft smooth shells, and buzzing beetles with brightly colored wings," said the boy.

"Then," said his mother, "you could tell me about each of the treasures you found, because you know about all kinds of interesting things."

Wise men store up knowledge.

Proverbs 10:14

"**When** we traveled through our kingdom, I would ride a tall white horse and carry a huge golden shield as I galloped ahead of your magnificent carriage," said the boy.

"And as we rode, all of the people would cheer and smile and wave," said his mother, "and you would smile and wave back, **because you are very friendly.**"

A cheerful look brings joy to the heart.
Proverbs 15:30

"**We** would see our friends in the marketplace," said the boy, "and visit the cobbler and the blacksmith and all of the merchants."

"And if one of those merchants dropped a gold coin," said his mother, "you would rush to pick it up and return it, because you do the right thing."

Therefore, as we have opportunity, let us do good to all people.

Galatians 6:10

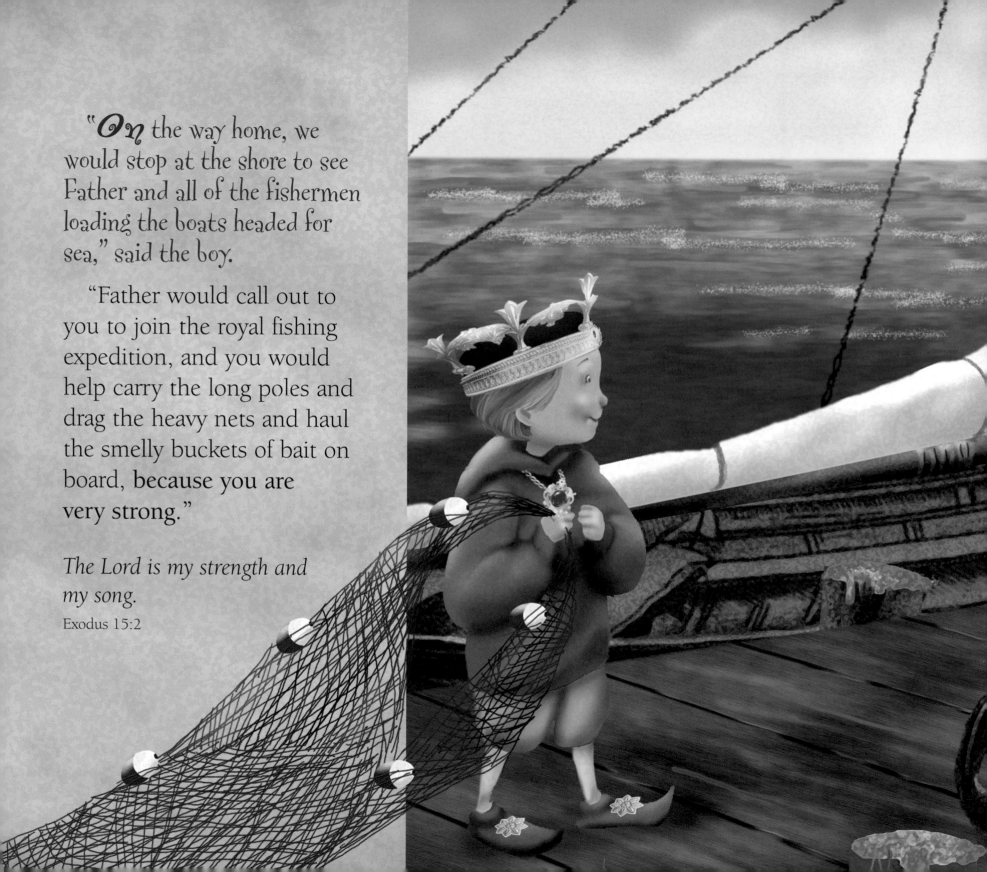

"**On** the way home, we would stop at the shore to see Father and all of the fishermen loading the boats headed for sea," said the boy.

"Father would call out to you to join the royal fishing expedition, and you would help carry the long poles and drag the heavy nets and haul the smelly buckets of bait on board, because you are very strong."

The Lord is my strength and my song.
Exodus 15:2

"We would bring all of the fish that I caught back to the castle to be food for a great celebration," said the boy. "I would invite everyone in our kingdom to join us."

"And when our guests arrived, you would welcome them into the castle," said his mother, "and share with them your games of chess and your set of wooden knights and horses, because you are very generous."

Be generous and willing to share.

1 Timothy 6:18

"**When** the feast was about to begin, all of our guests would gather in the great banquet hall and sit at long wooden tables filled with food," said the boy.

"And before we ate," said his mother, "Father would ask all of our guests to bow their heads. Then he would ask you to pray, giving thanks to the Lord for all of our blessings, because you love to talk to God."

Pray continually; give thanks in all circumstances.

1 Thessalonians 5:17, 18

"**At** nighttime we would read together by the fire in our castle's great hall," said the boy.

"I would read stories of brave knights going on mighty adventures," said his mother, "stories of heroes just like you. And you would listen carefully as I read, **because you are a good listener.**"

Let the wise listen and add to their learning.

Proverbs 1:5

"And after the story was over and I was sleepy, we would climb the grand staircase together to my room," said the boy.

"Then we would say our prayers together," said his mother. "In my prayers I would thank God for giving you to your father and me, because you are so very special."

Every good and perfect gift is from above.

James 1:17

"**Yes,** if you were a queen, I'd be your hero," the little boy said.

"**But** even if I am never a queen," said his mother, "and even if we never live in a gigantic castle, and even if I never ride in a magnificent carriage or attend a lavish feast, you will still be my hero forever and ever, because I love you so very much."

As I have loved you, so you must love one another.

John 13:34